Czerny 101 Exercises

Op. 261

Edited by ERNEST HAYWOOD

© 1930 Keith Prowse Music Ltd.
International Music Publications Ltd.
Griffin House 161 Hammersmith Road London W6 8BS England

101 EXERCISES

Edited by ERNEST HAYWOOD   ✵   CARL CZERNY, Op. 261

FINGER STUDY FOR THE RIGHT HAND

THE SAME FOR THE LEFT HAND

K. P. & Co. Ltd. 4352

SHORT PHRASING FOR THE RIGHT HAND

THE SAME FOR THE LEFT HAND

K. P. & Co Ltd 4352

7/5/15 all again next time/ quicker/ rests/ dynamics
FINGERING!

FOR EQUALIZING THE FINGERS OF THE RIGHT HAND

THE SAME FOR THE LEFT HAND

FOR DELICACY OF TOUCH

K. P. & Co. Ltd. 4352

STACCATO FOR THE RIGHT HAND

INDEPENDENCE AND EQUALITY FOR FINGERS OF THE RIGHT HAND

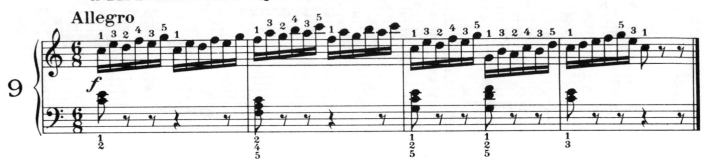

9

THE SAME FOR THE LEFT HAND

10

FINGER EQUALITY FOR THE RIGHT HAND

11

THE SAME FOR THE LEFT HAND

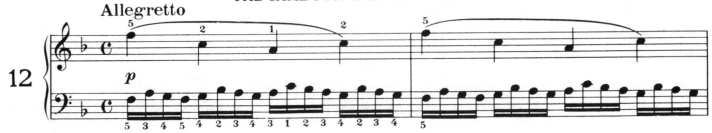

12

K. P. & Co. Ltd. 4352

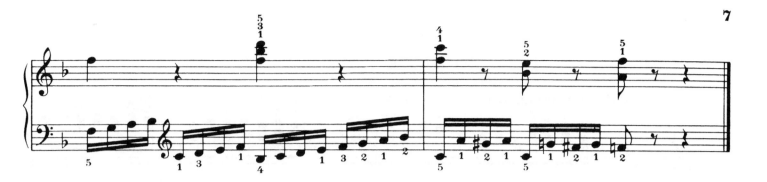

TO BE PLAYED WITH MINUET-LIKE GRACE

Allegretto con anima

13

8

STUDY ON DOUBLE NOTES, LEGATO AND STACCATO

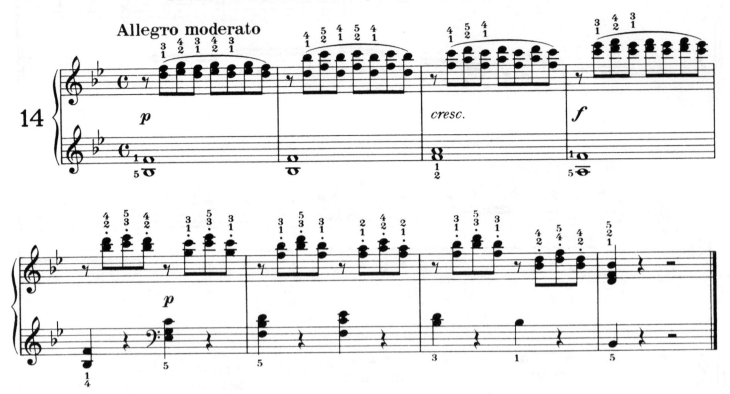

STUDY ON THIRDS, LEGATO AND STACCATO

UNANIMITY OF NOTE ATTACK IN BOTH HANDS

SHORT PIECE IN RONDINO STYLE

K. P. & Co. Ltd. 4352

STUDY IN STACCATO CHORDS

CHROMATIC GROUPS AND SCALES FOR THE RIGHT HAND

THE SAME FOR THE LEFT HAND

ON REPEATED NOTES

ON REPEATED NOTES

Allegretto vivace

22

STUDY IN THIRDS

THE SAME FOR THE RIGHT HAND ONLY

TO STRENGTHEN THE LEFT HAND

TO OBTAIN UNANIMITY IN EXECUTION OF THIRDS WITH BOTH HANDS

ON SCALE PASSAGES

PASSAGE OF THE THUMB IN RIGHT HAND ARPEGGIOS

K. P. & Co. Ltd. 4352

FOR LEGATO PLAYING

THE TURN

STACCATO NOTES AT COMMENCEMENT OF EACH GROUP

SHORT PHRASING

TO OBTAIN A TREMOLO IN BROKEN CHORDS

33

STUDY IN PART PLAYING

34

K. P. & Co. Ltd. 4352

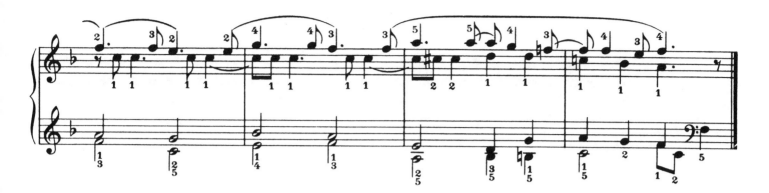

EXERCISE ON THE TURN FOR THE RIGHT HAND

PREPARATION FOR THE TRILL

ACCIACATURAS

ARPEGGIOS FOR THE RIGHT HAND

Allegro moderato

38

THE SAME FOR THE LEFT HAND

Allegro moderato

39

K. P. & Co. Ltd. 4352

LIGHTNESS AND GRACE

FOR STRENGTHENING THE TOUCH OF BOTH HANDS

K. P. & Co. Ltd. 4352

EXERCISE ON QUICK REPETITION OF SINGLE NOTES

FIRMNESS IN CHORD PLAYING

THE TRILL IN THE RIGHT HAND

Allegretto

44

THE TRILL IN THE LEFT HAND

Allegretto

45

PASSAGE WORK FOR THE LEFT HAND

LIGHT TOUCH AND LOOSENESS OF THE WRIST

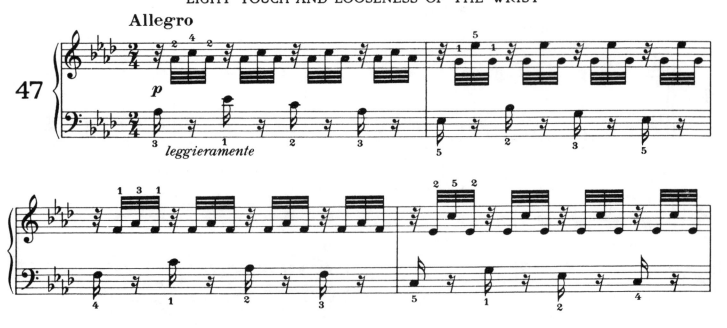

K. P. & Co. Ltd. 4352

PASSAGE WORK FOR BOTH HANDS

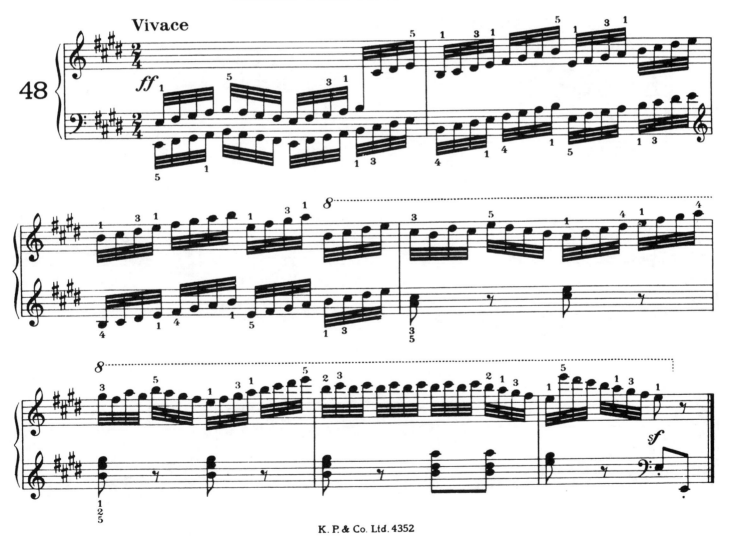

PART PLAYING

SHORT SCALE PASSAGES FOR EACH HAND

LEGATO CHANGE OF POSITION

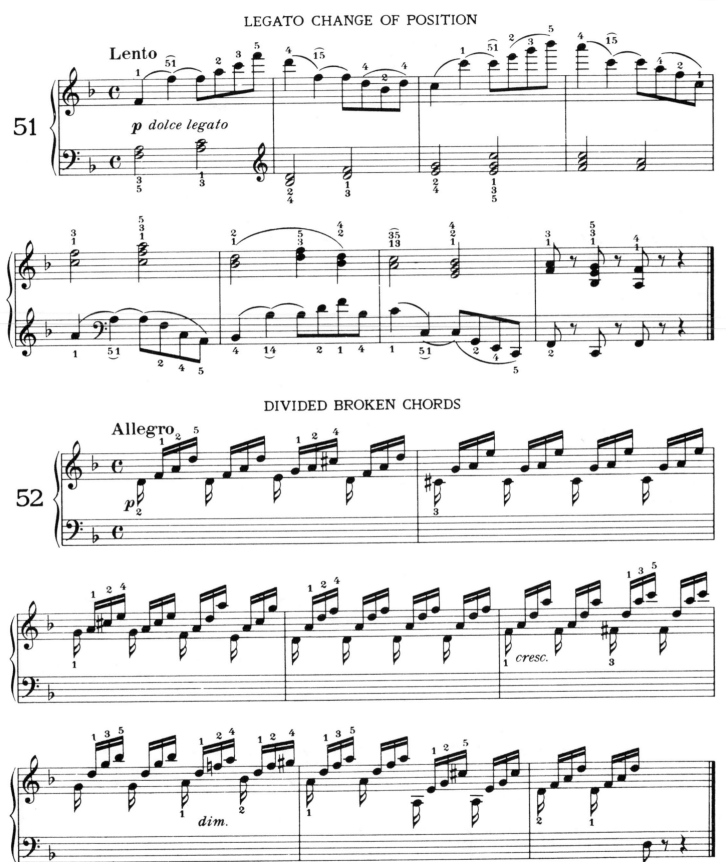

DIVIDED BROKEN CHORDS

THE SAME

53

FOR CROSSING THE HANDS

54

K. P & Co Ltd 4352

THE SAME

EQUALIZATION OF BOTH HANDS

K. P. & Co. Ltd. 4352

SUSTAINED CROTCHETS AGAINST MOVING SEMIQUAVERS

STUDY IN STACCATO CHORDS

K. P. & Co. Ltd. 4352

PASSAGE WORK FOR THE RIGHT HAND

FOR RAPID CHANGE OF POSITION OF THE RIGHT HAND

60

THE SAME FOR THE LEFT HAND

61

STUDY IN VARIED TOUCH FOR THE RIGHT HAND

62

K. P. & Co. Ltd. 4352

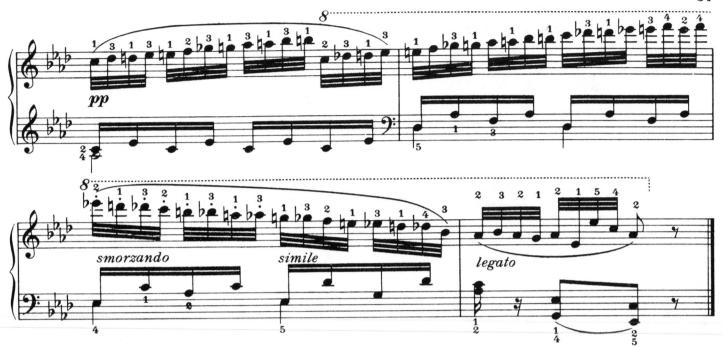

MELODY PLAYING WITH THE LITTLE FINGER OF RIGHT HAND

Allegro moderato

K. P. & Co Ltd. 4352

BROKEN CHROMATIC PASSAGES FOR THE LEFT HAND

REPEATED NOTES IN BOTH HANDS

K. P. & Co. Ltd. 4352

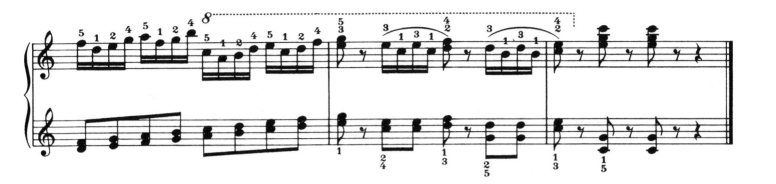

SUSTAINED NOTES WITH THE THUMB

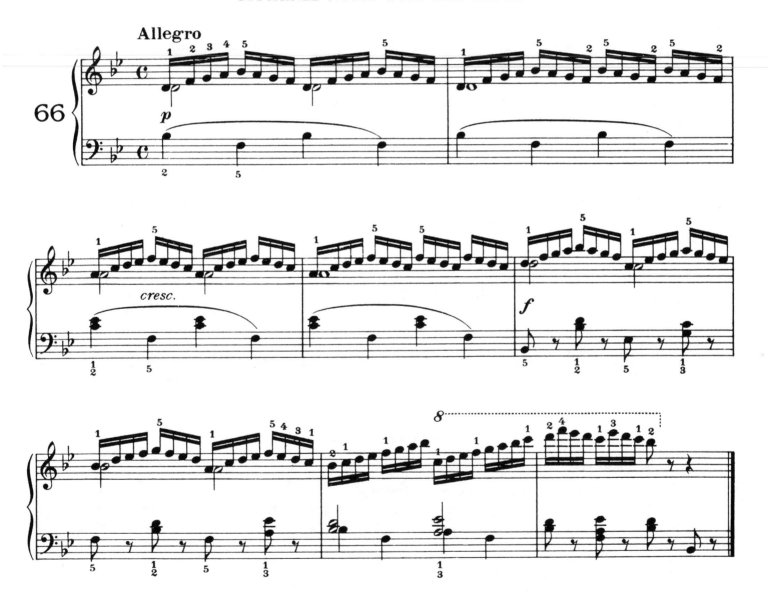

K. P. & Co. Ltd. 4352

THE PASSAGE OF 2ND FINGER OVER THUMB IN THE LEFT HAND

STACCATO LEAPS

STACCATO

PRACTICE IN TRIPLETS AND CHANGE OF POSITION

THE SAME FOR THE LEFT HAND

ARPEGGIOS FOR BOTH HANDS

BROKEN CHORDS FOR THE RIGHT HAND

SHORT PHRASING AND STACCATO

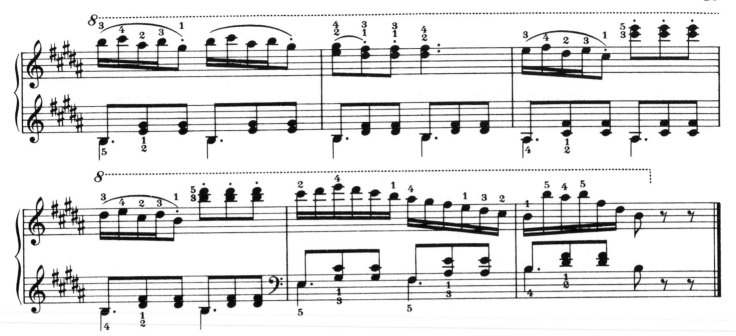

TO POINT A MELODY IN STACCATO THIRDS

Allegro

TO EQUALIZE THE TOUCH OF BOTH HANDS, ALSO AS A WRIST STUDY

STACCATO CHORDS

SCALE PASSAGE IN THIRDS

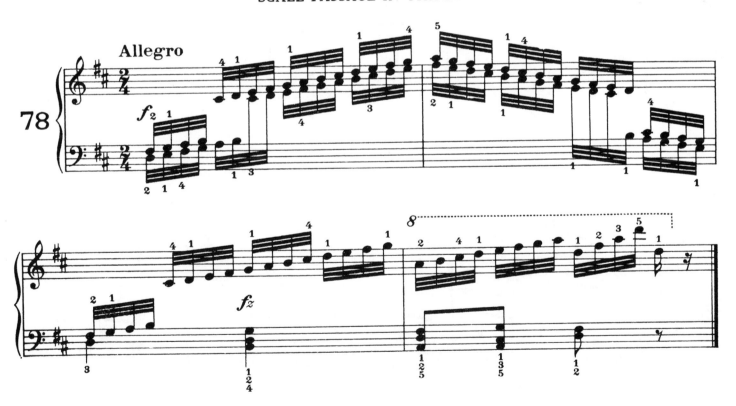

K. P. & Co. Ltd. 4352

THE MORDENTE AND THE TURN

THE TURN

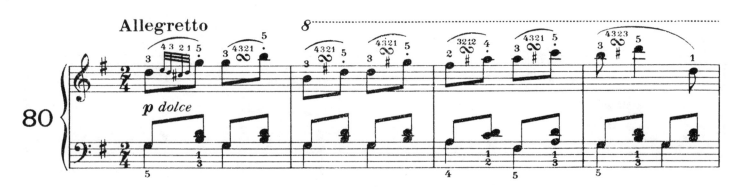

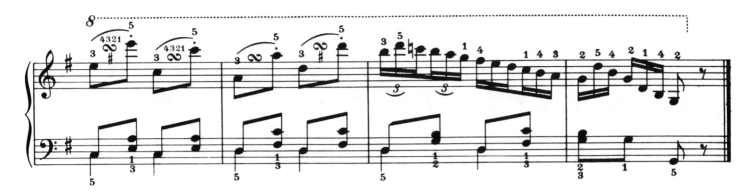

ARPEGGIOS DIVIDED BETWEEN THE HANDS

BROKEN ARPEGGIOS FOR THE RIGHT HAND

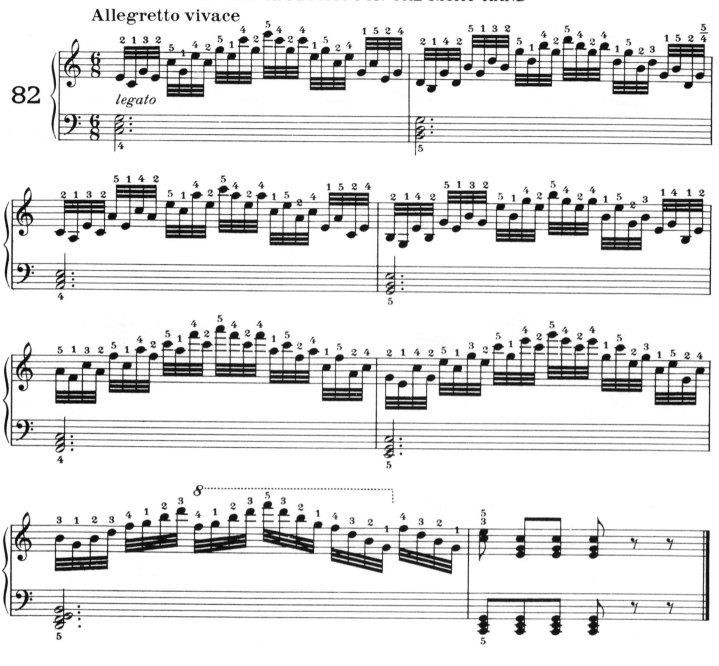

THE SAME FOR THE LEFT HAND

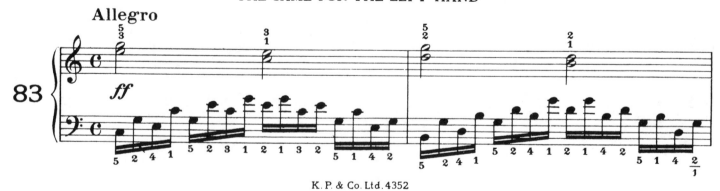

K. P. & Co. Ltd. 4352

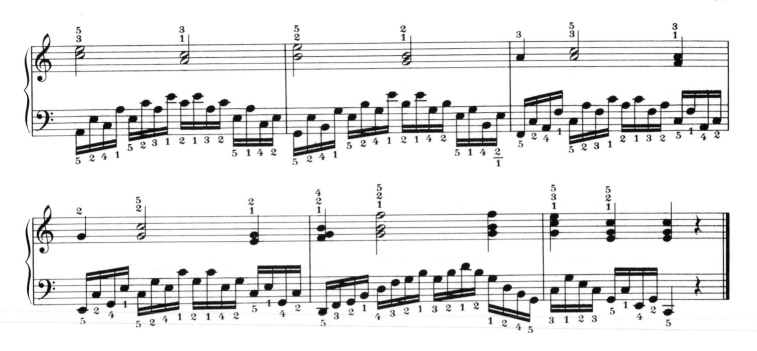

BROKEN ARPEGGIOS FOR BOTH HANDS

FOR REPETITION OF NOTES WITH THE SAME FINGER

ARPEGGIOS

STUDY IN LIGHTNESS OF TOUCH

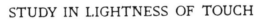

Allegretto

87

TREMOLO WITH SUSTAINED NOTES

INDEPENDENCE OF HANDS IN SUBDIVISION OF THE BEAT

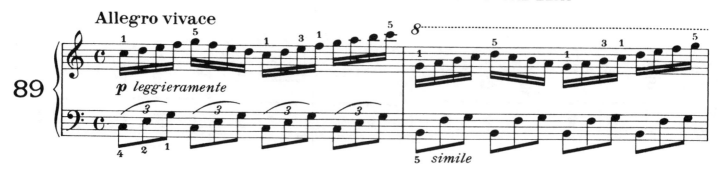

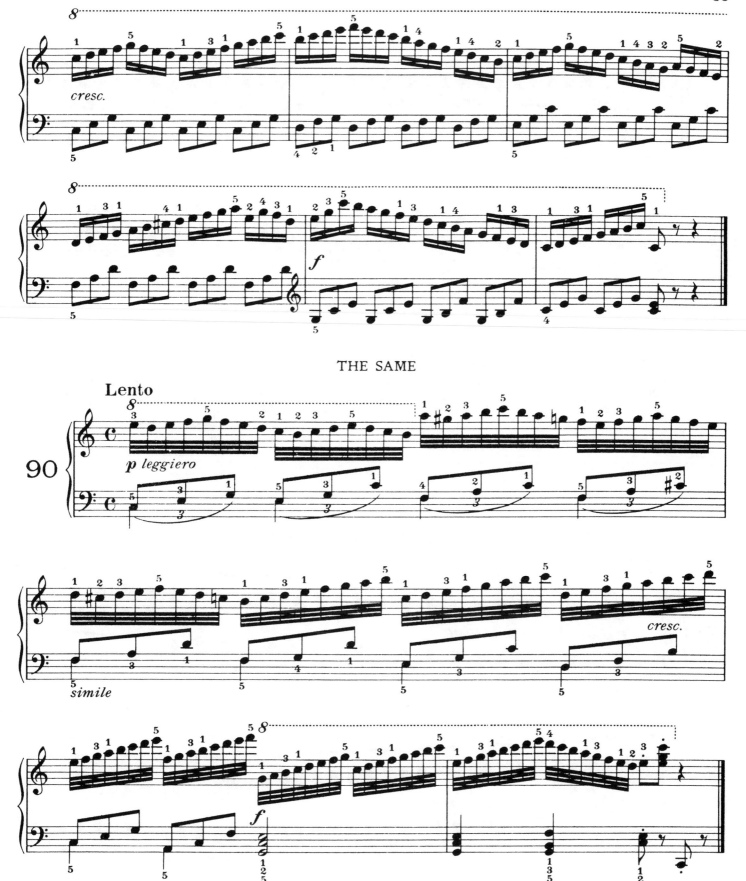

THE SAME

90 Lento

LEFT HAND OVER RIGHT HAND

91

DOUBLE THIRDS—BOTH HANDS

92

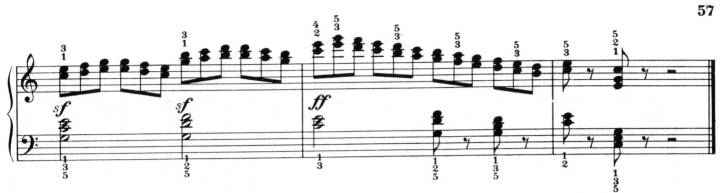

FLEXIBILITY AND LOOSENESS OF THE WRIST

PART PLAYING

TO STRENGTHEN AND EQUALIZE THE FINGERS OF BOTH HANDS

THE ACCOMPANIED TRILL

STUDY OF ORNAMENTAL PASSAGE WORK

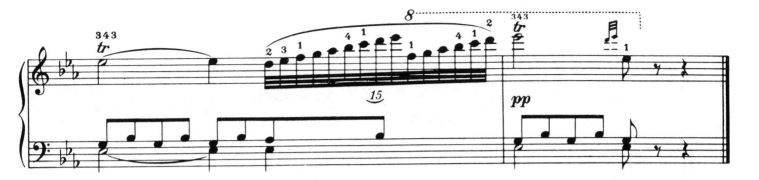

INDEPENDENCE OF THE HANDS

Allegro molto vivo

BROKEN ARPEGGIO PASSAGES FOR BOTH HANDS

SCALE PASSAGES FOR BOTH HANDS

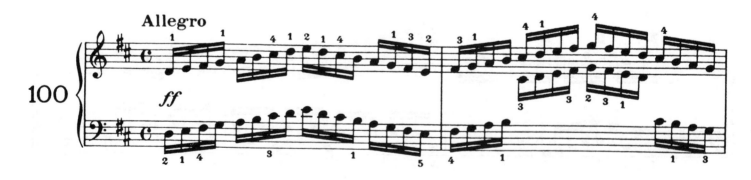

K. P. & Co. Ltd. 4352

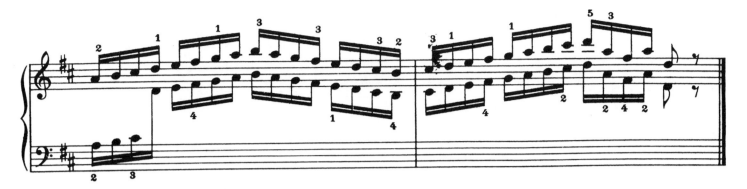

STACCATO CHORDS FOR THE RIGHT HAND

K. P. & Co. Ltd. 4352

Printed by
Halstan & Co. Ltd., Amersham, Bucks., England